# Contents

Meets **Accreditation Standard** for Child-created Bulletin Boards

# Introduction

This series of monthly activity books is designed to give PreK and Kindergarten teachers a collection of hands-on activities and ideas for each month of the year. The activities are standards-based and reflect the philosophy that children learn best through play. The teacher can use these ideas to enhance the development of language and math skills, and of social/emotional and physical growth of children. The opportunity to promote pre-reading skills is present throughout the series and should be incorporated whenever possible.

## Organization and Features

Each book consists of seven units:

**Unit 1** provides reproducible pages and information for the month in general.
- a newsletter outline to promote parent communication
- a blank thematic border page
- a list of special days in the month
- calendar ideas to promote math skills
- a blank calendar grid that can also be used as an incentive chart

**Units 2–6** include an array of activities for five **theme** topics. Each unit includes
- teacher information on the theme
- arts and crafts ideas
- a food activity
- poetry, songs, and books
- bulletin board ideas
- center activities correlated to specific learning standards

Implement the activities in a way that best meets the needs of individual children.

**Unit 7** focuses on a well-known **children's author**. The unit includes
- a biography of the author
- activities based on a literature selection
- a list of books by the author
- reproducible bookmarks

In addition, each book contains
- reproducible **icons** suitable to use as labels for centers in the classroom. The icons coordinate with the centers in the book. They may also be used with a work assignment chart to aid in assigning children to centers.
- reproducible **student awards**
- **calendar day pattern** with suggested activities

## Research Base

Howard Gardner's theory of multiple intelligences, or learning styles, validates teaching thematically and using a variety of approaches to help children learn. Providing a variety of experiences will assure that each child has an opportunity to learn in a comfortable way.

Following are the learning styles identified by Howard Gardner.
- **Verbal/Linguistic** learners need opportunities to read, listen, write, learn new words, and tell stories.
- **Musical** learners enjoy music activities.
- **Logical/Mathematical** learners need opportunities to problem solve, count, measure, and do patterning activities.
- **Visual/Spatial** learners need opportunities to paint, draw, sculpt, and create art works.
- **Interpersonal** learners benefit from group discussions and group projects.
- **Intrapersonal** learners learn best in solitary activities, such as reading, writing in journals, and reflecting on information.
- **Naturalist** learners need opportunities to observe weather and nature and to take care of animals and plants.
- **Existential** learners can be fostered in the early years by asking children to think and respond, by discussions, and by journal writing.

Gardner, H. (1994). *Frames of mind*. New York: Basic Books.

# May News

Teacher:_____

Date:_____

## Headline News

## Coming Up

## Happy Birthday to

## Special Thanks to

## Help Wanted

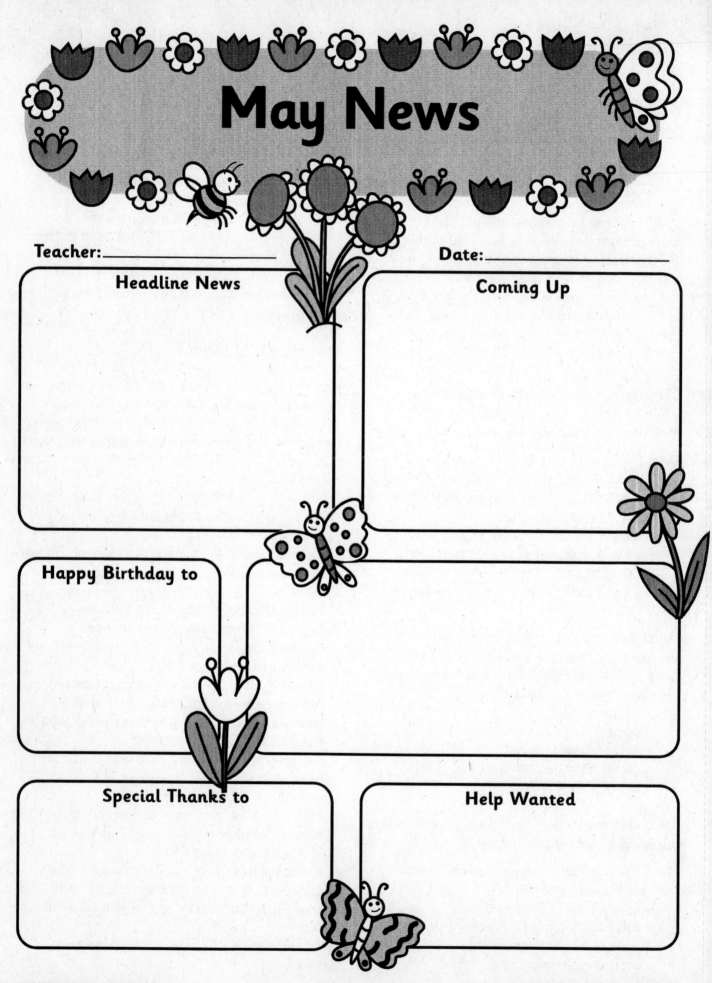

Three Cheers for May PreK–K, SV 9825-6

# May

Unit 1, Teacher Resources: Border Page

Three Cheers for May PreK–K, SV 9825-6

# Special Days in May

**American Bike Month** Challenge children to name the parts of a bicycle and have them describe their favorite place to ride their bike.

**Mother's Day** This special day falls on the second Sunday in May. Have children celebrate with activities from the Author Study unit that begins on page 85.

**1 Mother Goose Day** Select a familiar rhyme from a collection of Mother Goose poems. Have children take turns reciting the next line.

**1 Cheerios® Birthday (1941)** Read *The Cheerios Counting Book* by Barbara Barbieri McGrath (Scholastic). Have children practice counting from 1 to 10 and adding groups of ten using Cheerios.

**2 Brother/Sister Day** Have children dictate or write a sentence telling something they like to do with their brother or sister. For children that have no siblings, have them write about a close friend or relative.

**4 Space Day** Have children celebrate with activities from the Exploring Space unit that begins on page 10.

**4 National Kid's Fitness Day** Discuss with children the importance of exercise to stay fit and healthy. Encourage them to participate in several fitness exercises.

**5 Cinco de Mayo** Have children celebrate with activities from the Celebrate with Mexico unit that begins on page 71.

**8 No Socks Day** Invite children to wear shoes with no socks on this day.

**11 Jigsaw Day** Have a jigsaw puzzle competition. Have children work together in small groups to complete the puzzles.

**15 International Day of Families** Display pictures of families from other countries. Then invite children to draw a picture of their family and add it to the display.

**17 First Kentucky Derby (1875)** Invite children to bring a stick horse from home and have relay races.

**18 Mount Saint Helens Erupted (1980)** Have children learn about volcanoes with the science center activity on page 49.

**20 Strawberries Day** Read *The Little Mouse, the Red Ripe Strawberry, and the Big Hungry Bear* by Don Wood and Audrey Wood (Child's Play International, Ltd.). Bring strawberries to class. Have children cut a strawberry in half and share it with a friend.

**31 Memorial Day (observed)** Invite children to tell about someone in their family who is in the military. Then have them color a picture of the United States flag.

# May

| Sunday | Monday | Tuesday | Wednesday | Thursday | Friday | Saturday |
|--------|--------|---------|-----------|----------|--------|----------|
|        |        |         |           |          |        |          |
|        |        |         |           |          |        |          |
|        |        |         |           |          |        |          |
|        |        |         |           |          |        |          |
|        |        |         |           |          |        |          |

Unit 1, Teacher Resources: May Calendar
Three Cheers for May PreK–K, SV 9825-6

# Calendar Activities for May

## Classroom Calendar Setup

The use of the calendar in the classroom can provide children with daily practice on learning days, weeks, months, and years. As you plan the setup for your classroom, include enough space on the wall to staple a calendar grid labeled with the days of the week. Leave space above the grid for the name of the month and the year. Next to the calendar, staple twelve cards labeled with the months of the year and the number of days in each month. Leave these items on the wall all year. At the beginning of each month, start with the blank calendar grid. Do not staple anything on the grid that refers to the new month. Leave the days of the week and the year in place.

## Introducing the Month of May

Before children arrive, gather all of the items that will go on the calendar for May. You may want to include the following:

- name of the month
- number cards
- name cards to indicate birthdays during the month
- picture cards that tell about special holidays or school events during the month
- a small treat to be taped on the day of each child's birthday. You may wish to gift wrap the treat.

Add a special pointer that can be used each day while doing calendar activities. See page 9 for directions on how to make a pointer. Place these items in a picnic basket. Select a puppet that can remain in the basket and come out only to bring items for each new month. A dog puppet works well because of the large mouth which makes it easier to grasp each item.

On the first school day of the month, follow this procedure:

1. Place the picnic basket in front of the class. Pull out the puppet and introduce it to children if it is the first time they have seen it or ask them if they remember why the puppet is here. If this is the first time they have seen it, explain that the puppet will visit on the first day of each month to bring the new calendar items.

2. Have the puppet pull out the name of the month. According to the abilities of children, have them name the first letter in the name of the month, count the letters, or find the vowels. Staple the name of the month above the calendar.

3. Have the puppet pull out the new pointer for the teacher or the daily helper to use each day during calendar time.

4. Next, pull out the number cards for May. You may use plain number cards, cards made from the calendar day pattern on page 96, or seasonal die-cut shapes. By using two or three die-cut shapes, you can incorporate building patterns as part of your daily calendar routine. See page 9 for pattern ideas.

Three Cheers for May PreK–K, SV 9825-6

5. Place the number one card or die-cut under the day of the week on which May begins. Locate May on the month cards that are stapled next to your calendar. Have children tell how many days this month will have and then count that many spaces on the calendar to indicate the end of the month. You may wish to place a small stop sign as a visual reminder of the end of the month. Save the remaining numbers cards or die-cut shapes and add one each day.

6. If there are any birthdays during May, have the puppet pull out of the basket the cards that have a birthday symbol with the child's name and birth date written on it. Count from the number 1 to find where to staple this as a visual reminder of each child's birthday. If you have included a wrapped treat for each child, tape it on the calendar on the correct day.

7. Finally, have the puppet bring out cards that have pictures of holidays or special happenings, such as field trips, picture day, or story time in the library. Staple the picture cards on the correct day on the calendar grid. You can use these to practice various counting skills such as counting how many days until a field trip, a birthday, or a holiday.

8. When the basket is empty, say goodbye to the puppet and return it to the picnic basket. Put the basket away until the next month. Children will look forward to the beginning of each month in order to see what items the puppet will bring for the class calendar.

# Making a Flower Pointer

Include a flower pointer in the calendar basket for this month. To make a pointer, you will need the following:
- two 3" flower shapes cut from poster board
- a medium-sized dowel rod that is 18" long
- several 12" lengths of narrow purple and pink ribbon

## Directions:
1. Hot-glue the ribbons to the end of the dowel rod so that they lie against the rod.
2. Hot-glue the two flower shapes to the end of the dowel rod so that the flowers cover the glued ends of the ribbons.

The calendar helper can use this to point to the day of the week, the number, the month, and the year as the class says the date each day.

# Developing a Pattern

Practice patterning by writing the numbers 1–31 on die-cut shapes. You may want to use kite shapes in four different colors, such as green, yellow, orange, and purple. Write the numbers on the kite shapes in order using an ABCDABCD pattern. Have the children predict what color the kite will be on various days, such as the last day of the month.

# Exploring Space

 There are nine planets in our solar system. They are Mercury, Venus, Earth, Mars, Jupiter, Saturn, Uranus, Neptune, and Pluto.

 All of the planets revolve around the sun. It takes Earth 365 days to make a complete revolution around the sun.

 The sun is a star which is made up of burning gases. It provides our solar system with heat and light.

 There are billions of stars that vary in size and color in relation to the sun, which is a medium-sized, yellow star.

 Stars that are cooler than the sun are red, and stars that are hotter than the sun are blue.

 As it revolves around the sun, Earth also rotates every 24 hours.

 Earth has one moon that revolves around it approximately every month.

 The position of the moon in relation to Earth makes the phases of the moon.

 The moon is made of many of the same rock minerals that are found on Earth.

 The moon has about one sixth of the gravity of Earth.

 The American space program began in 1961, when Alan B. Shepard, Jr., became the first American astronaut to go into space.

 In July of 1969, Neil Armstrong was the first astronaut to walk on the moon.

Unit 2, Exploring Space: Teacher Information
Three Cheers for May PreK–K, SV 9825-6

# Moon Rover

## Materials

- pictures of a moon rover and an American flag on the surface of the moon
- 4 cups flour
- 2 cups salt
- water
- 6" paper plates
- toothpicks
- mini-marshmallows
- index cards cut into fourths
- glue
- markers or crayons
- bowl

## Directions

**Teacher Preparation:** Mix together salt and flour. Then add water until the dough has an elastic consistency.

Display the pictures. Discuss with children how the astronauts used a moon rover to explore the moon.

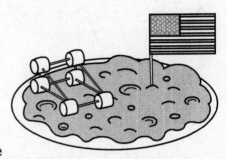

1. Press a 2" ball of dough flat to cover a paper plate. Make craters with fingers to resemble the surface of the moon.

2. Decorate the index card like the United States flag. Glue the edge of the flag to a toothpick and stand it in the dough.

3. Make a moon rover using the toothpicks and marshmallows. Place the moon rover on the surface of the moon.

# Tube Rocket

## Materials

- patterns on pages 19 and 20
- empty paper towel tubes
- 6-ounce paper cups
- foil
- black construction paper
- red, yellow, and orange crepe paper
- scissors
- glue
- masking tape
- stapler
- crayons

## Directions

**Teacher Preparation:** Duplicate a copy of the rocket pattern for each child. Make a template from the nose cone and fin patterns.

1. Cut out and color the rocket pattern. Wrap it around the paper towel tube and glue it in place.

2. Cover a paper cup with foil and attach the bottom end of the cup to the bottom end of the tube with masking tape.

3. Cut crepe paper into one-inch strips about one foot long. Staple or glue several strips inside the cup to resemble fire.

4. Trace the nose cone and two fin templates on black construction paper and cut them out.

5. Staple the sides of the nose cone pattern together to form a point and glue it to the top end of the tube.

6. Fold over a small section of the fins and apply glue. Attach the fins on opposite sides of the tube above the cup.

# Squishy Space Snack

## You will need

- dry instant pudding mix (one tablespoon per child)
- milk (three tablespoons per child)
- resealable plastic bags (quart size)
- measuring spoons
- scissors

## Directions

Discuss with children that astronauts experience zero gravity while in space and that even their food floats. Therefore, they have to eat some foods in an unusual way.

**Teacher Preparation:** Measure one tablespoon of dry pudding mix and three tablespoons of milk into a plastic bag for each child.

1. Squeeze bag with hands for about two minutes until ingredients are thoroughly mixed and mixture is smooth.

2. Cut off a very small piece of one corner of the bag.

3. Squeeze pudding into mouth like an astronaut.

Unit 2, Exploring Space: Kid's Kitchen
Three Cheers for May PreK–K, SV 9825-6

# 🎵 We're Going to Blast Off

(Tune: "Eensy Weensy Spider")

See the big space shuttle

On the launch pad.

The astronauts are ready,

And they are very glad

To put on their space suits

And climb aboard the ship.

Let's say the countdown

No number will we skip

**10, 9, 8, 7, 6, 5, 4, 3, 2, 1, 0, BLAST OFF!**

Have children squat slightly for each number in the countdown. They should be completely squatting for the number zero. Then have them jump up when they say "Blast off!"

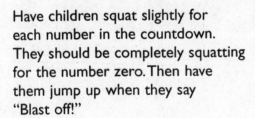

## Outer Space Stories

**Big Silver Space Shuttle**
by Ken Wilson-Max (Cartwheel Books)

**Floating in Space**
by Franklin M. Branely
(HarperCollins Juvenile Books)

**I Want to Be an Astronaut**
by Byron Barton (HarperCollins Juvenile Books)

**Looking into Space**
by Nigel Nelson (Reader's Digest)

**The Moon Book**
by Gail Gibbons (Holiday House)

**Papa, Please Get the Moon for Me**
by Eric Carle (Little Simon)

**The Planets in Our Solar System**
by Franklin M. Branely (HarperTrophy)

**There's No Place Like Space**
by Tish Babe (Random House Books
for Young Readers)

**Roaring Rockets**
by Tony Mitton (Turtleback Books)

# I Want to Be an Astronaut

## Materials

- pattern on page 21
- black craft paper
- 9" x 12" white construction paper
- clear dome lids from icy drinks
- photos of each child's face
- scissors
- glue
- white, yellow, red, orange tempera paints
- empty spray bottles
- border
- crayons
- stapler
- newspaper
- water

## Directions

**Teacher Preparation:** Cut black craft paper to the size of the bulletin board. Enlarge the pattern so that dome lid will be the correct size to cover the head. Duplicate a copy of the pattern on construction paper for each child. For each color of tempera paint, mix a small amount of paint with water in an empty spray bottle.

Read *I Want to Be an Astronaut* by Byron Barton (see book list on page 13) and discuss with children why astronauts wear space suits while working in space.

1. Lay black craft paper on a table or floor and surround with newspaper. Spray the paper with paint to resemble stars in space.

2. Staple the paper to the bulletin board.

3. Cut out the pattern and then cut out the face section. Decorate the space suit with a flag and the letters *USA*.

4. Glue a photo on the back side of the pattern so that the child appears to be the astronaut. Cover the photo with the clear dome lid and glue in place.

5. Staple astronauts in a pleasing arrangement on the bulletin board.

6. Add a border and the caption.

**Tip:** Ask your local fast food restaurant to donate the clear dome lids.

# Exploring Space Centers

### Art Center

**Language Arts Standard**
Writes labels and captions

## The Sun Is Our Star

### Materials

- paper plates
- black marker
- yellow tempera paint
- orange construction paper
- glue
- scissors
- paintbrushes

**Teacher Preparation:** Cut a generous supply of construction paper into 1" x 6" strips.

Lead children in a discussion about the sun as the closest star to Earth. Explain that stars are made of hot, burning gases. Invite children to glue orange paper strips around the edge of the front side of a paper plate. Then have them turn the plate over and paint the back yellow. Allow to dry and have children use the marker to write the word *sun* on the plate.

**Extension:** Encourage children to write the sentence *The sun is a star* on the plate or on a sheet of paper.

### Block Center

**Science Standard**
Understands about scientific inquiry

## Traveling in Space

### Materials

- 2 or 3 large balloons
- rockets made in "Tube Rocket" on page 11
- pictures of a rocket launch and of the planets
- yarn
- wooden building blocks

**Teacher Preparation:** Blow up balloons as planets and tie a length of yarn to each one. Hang the balloons from the ceiling so they are slightly above eye level for children. Display pictures in the block center.

Lead children in a discussion about space travel and the planets. Invite them to use blocks to build a launch pad for the rockets that they made on page 11. Then have them count down and move the rockets to blast off and travel around the planets.

Three Cheers for May PreK–K, SV 9825-6

# Exploring Space Centers

## Dramatic Play Center

**Social Studies Standard**
Understands the importance of jobs

## Working in Space

### Materials

- gallon milk jugs
- large nuts and bolts
- hot glue gun
- garden gloves
- elastic
- 3-liter soda bottles
- appliance box
- duct tape
- matte knife

**Teacher Preparation:** Open both ends of the appliance box so that children can crawl through it. Make several holes on the side of the box so that the bolts can be inserted through them. Secure the head of the bolts with duct tape on the inside of the box. Partially screw the nuts onto the bolts. Cut away the handle and pouring section of the milk jug with the matte knife to make a helmet. Glue two empty soda bottles together for air tanks. Use duct tape to attach two pieces of elastic to the bottles to make shoulder straps.

Explain to children that sometimes it is necessary for astronauts to repair the spaceship, a satellite, or the space station. Tell children that astronauts wear space suits when they leave the spaceship to make repairs. Invite children to role-play astronauts by wearing a helmet, gloves, and an oxygen tank and crawling through the box to repair the spaceship. Have them screw the nuts on the bolts.

## Game Center

**Math Standard**
Associates numerals up to 10 with sets of objects

## Collecting Moon Rocks

### Materials

- pair of tongs
- 20–30 rocks (about 1" to 2" in size)
- a die
- a large butter tub

Tell children that astronauts use a tong-like tool to pick up moon rocks. Invite children to take turns rolling the die to determine how many rocks they can collect. Have children use tongs to pick up rocks and place them in the butter tub. Tell children to continue rolling the die until all of the rocks are collected.

# Exploring Space Centers

## Language Center

**Language Arts Standard**
Recognizes and names uppercase and lowercase letters correctly

## Rocket Letter Cards

### Materials

- crayons
- cards on page 22
- glue
- scissors
- construction paper

**Teacher Preparation:** Duplicate a picture card for each letter of the alphabet. Write one uppercase or lowercase letter on each card. Glue cards to construction paper and cut them out.

Invite children to play with a partner. One partner will stack the letter cards and display the card on top of the deck. If the other partner can name the letter, that child may keep it in his or her stack. If he or she cannot name the letter, the card is returned to the bottom of the stack. Have children continue playing as they take turns naming the letters.

## Math Center

**Math Standard**
Counts backwards from 10 to 1

## Count Down to Blast Off

### Materials

- pattern on page 22
- yellow construction paper
- scissors
- magnetic board
- black marker
- magnetic tape

**Teacher Preparation:** Duplicate eleven copies of the pattern on yellow construction paper. Write a number from 0 to 10 on each star and then cut them out. Attach magnetic tape to the back of each star.

Discuss with children that mission control counts backwards from 10 to 0 right before liftoff occurs. Have children arrange the stars in numerical order backwards from 10 to 0 on the magnetic board. Then have children stand and count backwards from 10 to 0. For each number, have them squat a little closer to the floor. When they get to zero, have them jump up and say in a loud voice, "Blast Off!"

# Exploring Space Centers

## Science Center

**Science Standard**
Understands about scientific inquiry

## Straw Rockets

### Materials

- tape
- markers
- large and small drinking straws
- scissors
- index cards
- modeling clay

**Teacher Preparation:** Cut index cards in half.

Have children draw a picture of a rocket on an index card and cut it out. Have them tape the rocket to one end of the large straw. Then have them plug the same end of the straw with a pea-size ball of modeling clay. Have children insert a small drinking straw halfway into the open end of the large straw. Invite children to blow through the small straw to launch the rocket.

## Writing Center

**Language Arts Standard**
Makes illustrations to match sentences

## My Space Book

### Materials

- stapler
- construction paper
- activity masters on pages 23 and 24
- pencils
- crayons

**Teacher Preparation:** Duplicate and cut apart the booklet masters. Make covers from construction paper and assemble the books. Provide a booklet for each child.

Read the booklet and have children follow along. Then have them trace the words on each page and illustrate the sentences. Invite children to decorate the cover.

# Rocket Pattern

Use with "Tube Rocket" on page 11.

**rocket**

# Nose Cone and Fin Patterns

Use with "Tube Rocket" on page 11.

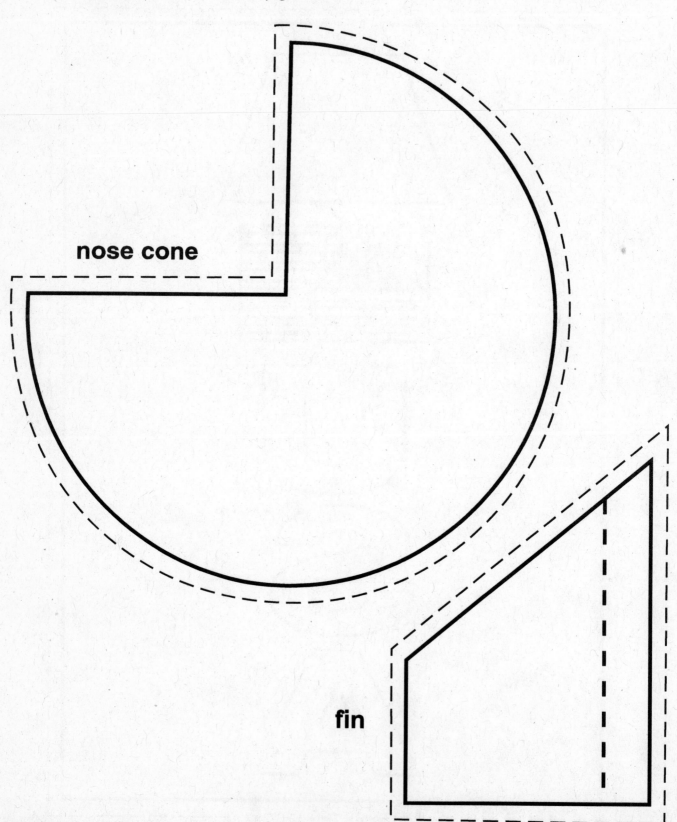

nose cone

fin

Unit 2, Exploring Space: Patterns
Three Cheers for May PreK–K, SV 9825-6

# Astronaut Pattern

Use with "I Want to Be an Astronaut" on page 14.

**astronaut**

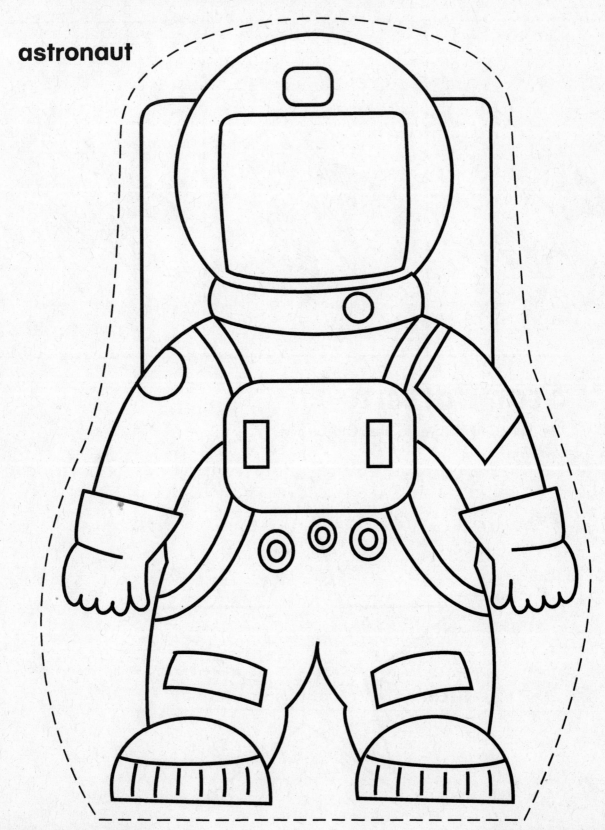

Three Cheers for May PreK–K, SV 9825-6

# Picture Cards

Use with "Rocket Letter Cards" on page 17.

# Star Pattern

Use with "Count Down to Blast Off" on page 17.

star

# Booklet Activity Master

Use with "My Space Book" on page 18.

The _____stars_____ are hot.

1

The _____sun_____ is yellow.

2

Three Cheers for May PreK–K, SV 9825-6

# Booklet Activity Master

Use with "My Space Book" on page 18.

The __moon__ is a rock.

3

I love the __Earth__.

4

Three Cheers for May PreK–K, SV 9825-6

# Magnificent Monarchs

 The monarch is a flying insect with large scaly wings. Monarchs have six jointed legs, three body parts (a head, thorax, and an abdomen), a pair of antennae, compound eyes, and an exoskeleton.

 Female monarchs lay one ridged, spherical egg under the leaf of a milkweed plant. The egg hatches in 3–5 days.

 The larva (caterpillar) hatches from the egg and eats the shell. Then the black, white, and yellow caterpillar eats milkweed leaves and molts, or sheds its outer skin, four times as it grows. Each time it molts, the caterpillar eats its outer skin.

 The milkweed leaves that the caterpillar eats are poisonous, which makes the caterpillar poisonous to predators. These animals get very sick and vomit.

 When the caterpillar is about two inches long, it finds a protected branch and turns into a jade green pupa, or chrysalis. It hangs upside down and molts for the last time. In 10–12 days the chrysalis becomes transparent.

 During this time metamorphosis has occurred, and the adult emerges from the chrysalis. The damp, folded wings are black and orange with white dots. The butterfly can now eat only liquids through a straw-like mouth called a proboscis.

 Just as it was in the larva stage, the adult monarch is poisonous to predators. These animals remember this brightly colored butterfly made them sick and avoid all monarchs in the future.

 Monarchs are found all across North America. Some groups of monarchs migrate in the fall thousands of miles to the mountains in Central Mexico and back again in the spring. They are the only butterflies that make such a long, two-way migration every year.

 The life span of the adult monarch varies depending on when it emerged from the pupa. The earlier in the season the adult emerged, the shorter the life span. The life span ranges from 2–5 weeks to 8–9 months.

# ...ycle Headband

- glue
- stapler
- scissors
- large green pom-poms

- black, yellow, and white pom-poms

- crayons or markers

## Directions

**Teacher Preparation:** Duplicate a copy of the patterns for each child.

1. Color one leaf pattern green. Cut it out and glue one bead on the leaf. Glue the leaf on a sentence strip.

2. Color the second leaf pattern green and cut it out. Tear away a small section of the leaf as if a caterpillar ate it. Glue six pom-poms on the leaf in a black, yellow, white pattern to resemble a caterpillar. Glue the leaf on the sentence strip.

3. Glue a large green pom-pom on the sentence strip to resemble the chrysalis.

4. Color the butterfly to resemble a monarch. Cut it out and glue it on the sentence strip.

5. Staple the ends of the sentence strip together to make a headband.

# Butterfly Windsock

## Materials

- patterns on page 35
- lunch sacks (one per child)
- crepe paper
- crayons or markers

- scissors
- glue
- yarn
- hole punch

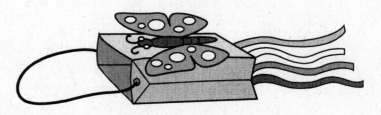

## Directions

**Teacher Preparation:** Duplicate the patterns to provide two wings and one body pattern for each child. Cut off the bottom end of the lunch sacks. Provide a lunch sack for each child.

1. Cut several crepe paper streamers to the desired length. Glue the streamers around the inside edge of one end of the sack.

2. Color and cut out the wings and the body patterns. Glue the wings to the body.

3. Glue the butterfly to one side of the lunch sack, positioning it so that the streamers are at the bottom end of the body.

4. Punch holes on both sides of the bag at the top end. Tie a piece of yarn through each hole.

5. Take the windsock outside and hold it high to let the wind blow through it.

# Butterfly Brunch

## You will need

- bread (one slice per child)
- softened cream cheese
- food coloring
- round crackers
- pretzel sticks
- raisins
- carrots
- bread knife
- plastic knives
- paper plates

## Directions

**Teacher Preparation:** Trim the crust from bread slices to form a square. Provide one slice per child. Then cut each slice diagonally to form two triangles. Stir a few drops of food coloring into the softened cream cheese for desired color. Slice carrots into thin circles.

1. Lay three crackers in a row in the center of the plate to make the three parts of the butterfly's body.

2. Stick two raisins on the top cracker with a dab of cream cheese to make the eyes.

3. Spread cream cheese on the bread. Then place the bread triangles on the plate with the top of the triangles touching the crackers to form the wings.

4. Lay two pretzels above the top cracker for the antennae.

5. Decorate the wings with carrot slices. Encourage children to make the wings symmetrical like a butterfly's wings.

Three Cheers for May PreK–K, SV 9825-6

# 🎵 The Butterfly Song

(Tune: "Up on the Housetop")

First comes a butterfly that lays an egg.

Out comes a caterpillar with many legs.

Oh, see the caterpillar spin and spin

A little chrysalis to sleep in.

Oh, oh, oh, see it change!

Oh, oh, oh, see it change!

Out of the chrysalis—my, oh, my.

Out comes a pretty butterfly.

## Beautiful Butterfly Books

**A Monarch Butterfly's Life**
by John Himmelman (Children's Press)

**The Butterfly Alphabet Book**
by Brian Cassie (Charlesbridge Publishing)

**The Butterfly House**
by Eve Bunting (Scholastic Books)

**The Crunching, Munching Caterpillar**
by Sheridan Cain (Tiger Tales)

**Gotta Go! Gotta Go!**
by Sam Swope (Farrar Straus & Giroux)

**Monarch Butterfly**
by Gail Gibbons (Holiday House)

**The Very Hungry Caterpillar**
by Eric Carle (Scholastic Books)

**Waiting for Wings**
by Lois Ehlert (Harcourt Children's Books)

Three Cheers for May PreK–K, SV 9825-6

# Monarch Migration

## Materials

- patterns on page 35
- green craft paper
- spoons
- scissors
- black and white construction paper
- black and orange tempera paints
- stapler
- white crayon

## Directions

**Teacher Preparation:** Cover the bulletin board with craft paper. Duplicate the wing and body patterns to make templates. Enlarge if desired. Provide each child with a template.

1. Trace the body template on black construction and cut it out. Draw two eyes on the head with the white crayon.

2. Fold the white construction paper in half. Then place the straight edge of the wing template on the fold and trace. Cut out the wing through the two thicknesses.

3. Open the folded paper. Place spoonfuls of black and orange paint on one side of the butterfly shape. Position more of the orange paint in the center and the black paint closer to the edge.

4. Close the folded paper and rub over the paper with fingers so that the paint is smoothed out. Open to reveal two symmetrical wings of a monarch butterfly.

5. Glue the body to the center of the wings.

6. Staple the butterflies close together on the board to resemble monarchs in the mountains of Mexico. Add a border and caption.

**Note:** See *Monarch Butterfly* by Gail Gibbons for more information and pictures.

# Magnificent Monarchs Centers

### Art Center

**Science Standard**
Understands the characteristics of organisms

## Butterfly Wings

### Materials

- black markers
- orange and white tempera paints
- 12" x 18" black construction paper
- stapler
- scissors
- paintbrushes

**Teacher Preparation:** Cut out two large wings and a large body similar to the pattern on page 35 for each child to wear. Cut 2" x 18" strips for shoulder straps.

Invite children to glue the two wings to the body. Then have them paint the wings with orange paint, leaving the outside edge black. Invite children to paint white dots on the black edges. Allow the paint to dry. Have children draw veins with the black marker. Staple two paper strips on the back of the butterfly for shoulder straps. These wings may be used in the dramatic play center below.

### Dramatic Play Center

**Language Arts Standard**
Sequences events accurately

## Singing Butterflies

### Materials

- paper or plastic flowers
- small blankets or towels
- butterfly wings made in "Butterfly Wings" on this page

Follow the directions listed in the art center above for making butterfly wings. Then teach children "The Butterfly Song" on page 28 and have them role-play the song. Invite children to crawl like a caterpillar and wrap up in a blanket like a chrysalis. Have them wear the butterfly wings and fly from flower to flower.

# Magnificent Monarchs Centers

## Language Center

**Language Arts Standard**
Recognizes and names uppercase and lowercase letters

## Wings That Match

### Materials

- 6 plastic milk caps
- pattern on page 36
- crayons or markers
- glue
- scissors
- file folder

**Teacher Preparation:** Duplicate and color the butterfly. Cut it out and glue it on the inside of a file folder. Write a lowercase letter on each circle on the butterfly wings. Write the corresponding capital letters on the plastic milk caps.

Have children match the capital letters to the lowercase letters.

**Extension:** For a phonemic awareness activity, draw or cut out pictures whose names have the same beginning sounds as the letters used. Glue the pictures on the milk caps. Have children match the letters with beginning sounds.

## Math Center

**Math Standard**
Associates numerals up to 10 with sets of objects

## Butterfly Count

### Materials

- construction paper
- markers or crayons
- 55 small plastic butterflies
- glue
- scissors
- pattern on page 37

**Teacher Preparation:** Duplicate and color ten copies of the math board. Cut them out and glue them to construction paper for durability. Write a number from 1 to 10 on each math board.

Invite children to count the corresponding number of butterflies and place them on each math board.

**Tip:** Most party stores have inexpensive plastic butterflies that can be used for this activity.

# Magnificent Monarchs Centers

### Music Center

## Dancing Butterflies

### Materials

- colorful scarves
- music with different tempos

Have children use the scarves as wings and dance to the beat of the music.

**Extension:** To practice position words, have children move like butterflies and go to a specific spot in the room. For example, have them fly *behind* the door or *between* the desks.

### Reading Center

## Colorful Butterflies

### Materials

- construction paper
- crayons or markers
- patterns on pages 34 and 38
- glue
- scissors

**Teacher Preparation:** Duplicate, color, and cut out the word cards. Duplicate eight copies of the butterfly on page 34 and color each one to match one of the colors on the word cards. Glue the word cards and butterflies to construction paper for durability.

Read *The Butterfly Alphabet Book* by Brian Cassie. Discuss with children the different colors seen on the butterflies. Have children match the word card to the butterfly of the corresponding color.

# Magnificent Monarchs Centers

### Science Center

**Science Standard**
Understands characteristics
of organisms

## From Egg to Butterfly

### Materials

- wet cotton balls
- magnifying glass
- milkweed plants
- crayons
- bug cage
- monarch caterpillars

**Teacher Preparation:** Order monarch caterpillars online at www.monarchwatch.org. The company only ships to areas east of the Rockies where milkweed grows. Painted Lady caterpillars can be ordered online at www.insectlore.com if monarch caterpillars are not available in your area. Keep milkweed leaf stems in wet cotton balls. Replace milkweed with fresh plants as needed and keep the cotton ball wet during the larva stage.

Have children use the magnifying glass to observe the caterpillars and draw a picture of what they see. Repeat the activity with the chrysalis and the adult butterfly.

### Writing Center

**Language Arts Standard**
Writes words that move from
left to right

## Butterfly Words

### Materials

- scissors
- construction paper
- activity masters on pages 39 and 40
- pencils
- stapler
- crayons

**Teacher Preparation:** Duplicate and cut apart the booklet masters. Make covers from the construction paper and assemble the booklets. Provide a booklet for each child.

Write the word *Butterfly* on the chalkboard and have children copy it on the cover. Invite children to open the booklet and read along with you. Have children use their fingers to trace the word on each page. In the center, have children use a pencil to trace the letters and color the picture.

# Leaf and Butterfly Patterns

Use with "Monarch Life Cycle Headband" on page 26 and "Colorful Butterflies" on page 32.

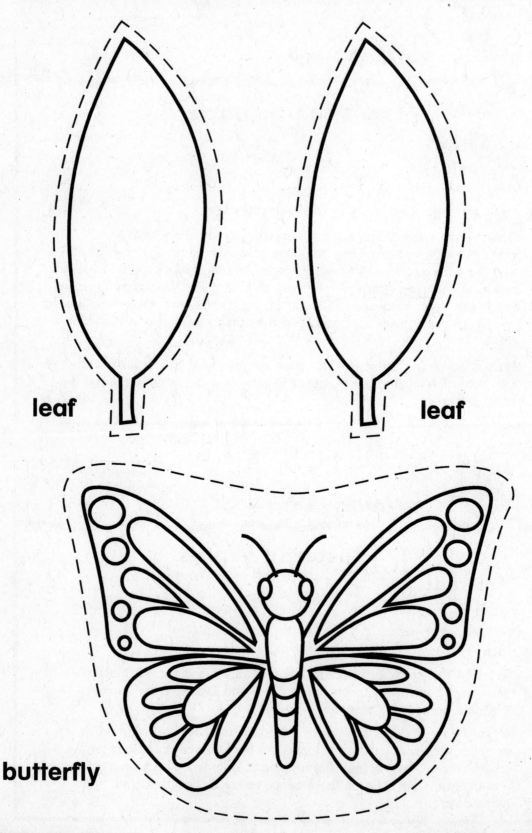

leaf

leaf

butterfly

Unit 3, Magnificent Monarchs: Patterns
Three Cheers for May PreK–K, SV 9825-6

# Wing and Body Patterns

Use with "Butterfly Windsock" on page 26 and "Monarch Migration" on page 29.

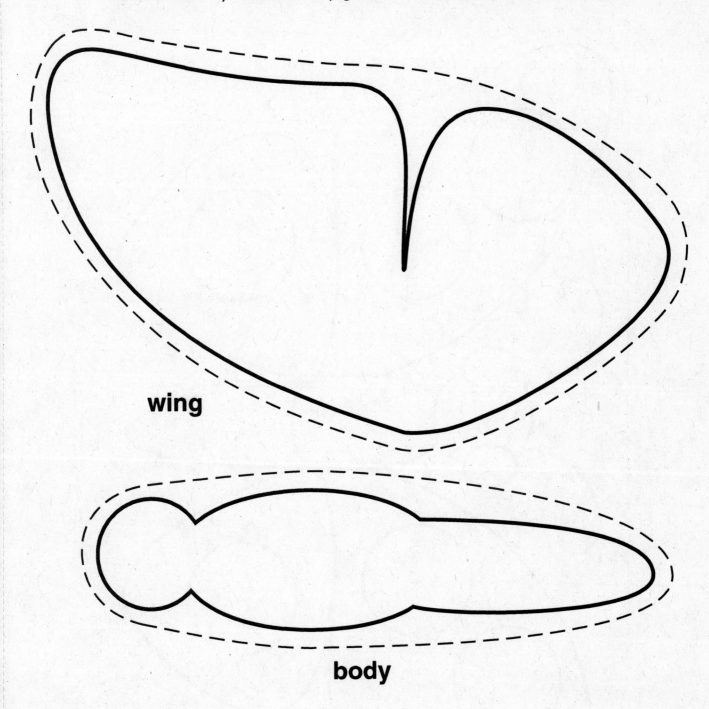

wing

body

Three Cheers for May PreK–K, SV 9825-6

# Butterfly Pattern

Use with "Wings That Match" on page 31.

Unit 3, Magnificent Monarchs: Patterns
Three Cheers for May PreK–K, SV 9825-6

# Math Board Pattern

Use with "Butterfly Count" on page 31.

# Word Cards

Use with "Colorful Butterflies" on page 32.

yellow

green

purple

black

red

blue

orange

brown

Unit 3, Magnificent Monarchs: Cards
Three Cheers for May PreK–K, SV 9825-6

# Booklet Activity Master

Use with "Butterfly Words" on page 33.

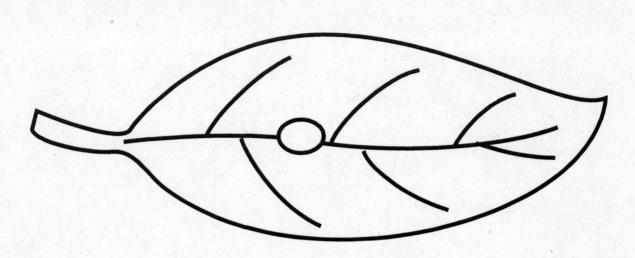

egg

1

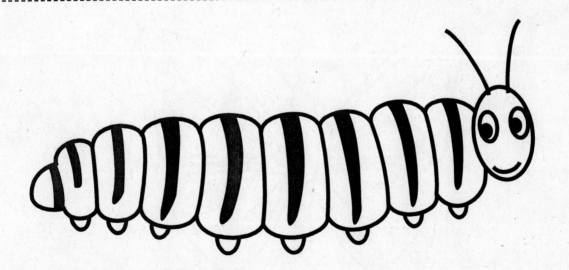

caterpillar

2

**39**

# Booklet Activity Master

Use with "Butterfly Words" on page 33.

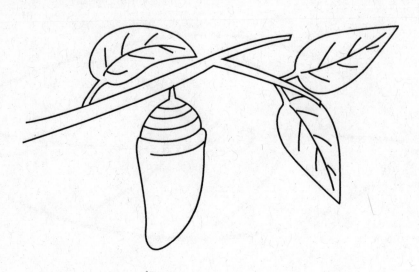

chrysalis

3

butterfly

4

Unit 3, **Magnificent Monarchs: Activity Master**
Three Cheers for May PreK–K, SV 9825-6

# Rocks Are Everywhere

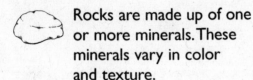 Rocks are made up of one or more minerals. These minerals vary in color and texture.

Rocks are constantly being changed by the environment. This is called the rock cycle.

Rocks are classified according to how they are formed. There are three kinds of rock: igneous, sedimentary, and metamorphic.

*Igneous* means made from fire or heat. When a volcano erupts, the magma or hot lava spills out on the surface and cools. The magma turns from a liquid to a solid to form igneous rocks.

Sometimes the magma cools quickly and traps gas bubbles inside to form a rock called pumice. It is the only rock that floats.

Sedimentary rocks are formed by layers of sediments from sand, mud, animal material, or plant material. Fossils of animals and plants are found in sedimentary rocks.

Seventy percent of all rocks on the Earth's surface are sedimentary.

Metamorphic rocks are formed by adding heat and pressure to igneous or sedimentary rocks. The heat and pressure change the rock formation.

Geodes are fascinating geological formations. A geode is a spherical lump with a hollow cavity filled with crystals.

Rock crystals are transparent crystalline minerals that form a definite shape.

Three Cheers for May PreK–K, SV 9825-6

# Pet Rocks

## Materials

- a rock for each child
- tempera paints
- paintbrushes
- wiggly eyes
- black fine-tip permanent markers
- pom-poms
- fake fur fabric
- glue
- scissors

## Directions

**Teacher Preparation:** Collect rocks of different shapes and sizes that are smooth enough to paint. You may wish to have children bring a rock from home for this activity.

1. Paint rocks the desired colors. Allow paint to dry.

2. Glue on two wiggly eyes and draw a nose and mouth with the marker.

3. Cut a small piece of fake fur and glue it on the rock for hair.

4. Glue on a pom-pom for a tail.

5. Name your rock.

# Rock Ring

## Materials

- metal bottle caps (not twist caps)
- twist-ties
- glue
- awl (small pointed tool for making holes in bottle caps)
- hammer
- aquarium rocks

## Directions

**Teacher Preparation:** Use the hammer and awl to make two holes in each bottle cap. Insert the two ends of the twist-tie through the holes on the top side of the cap. Leave a finger-sized loop on the top. Turn the cap over and twist the ends together to secure the loop.

1. Fill the bottle cap with a layer of glue. Cover the glue with aquarium rocks.

2. Add another layer of glue and more rocks. Repeat, if desired.

3. Allow to dry and wear the ring.

Three Cheers for May PreK–K, SV 9825-6

# Sedimentary Sandwiches

## You will need

- one slice of whole wheat bread per child
- one slice of white bread per child
- softened cream cheese
- grape jelly
- apricot jam
- strawberry jelly
- paper plates
- napkins
- plastic knives
- spoons

## Directions

**Teacher Preparation:** Lead children in a discussion about how sedimentary rocks are formed by layers on top of layers. Tell children that sometimes plant or animal fossils are part of the layers. Provide each child with a slice of wheat bread and a slice of white bread. Place a generous spoonful of each jelly, the jam, and the cream cheese on a paper plate.

1. Use the plastic knife to spread a thick layer of each ingredient on one slice of bread. Repeat layers if desired.

2. Top with the second slice of bread. Cut the sandwich in half and count the layers. Look for strawberry "fossils."

3. Eat the layered sandwich. Yum!

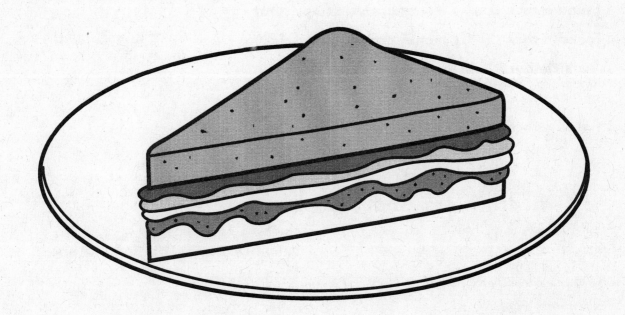

Three Cheers for May PreK–K, SV 9825-6

# 🎵 I Found a Rock

(Tune: "If You're Happy and You Know It")

I found a rock that is igneous. (clap, clap)

I found a rock that is igneous. (clap, clap)

It came from a volcano

And was made by heat and fire.

I found a rock that is igneous. (clap, clap)


I found a rock that is sedimentary. (clap, clap)

I found a rock that is sedimentary. (clap, clap)

It has many, many layers

Of fossils, sand, and mud.

I found a rock that is sedimentary. (clap, clap)


I found a rock that is metamorphic. (clap, clap)

I found a rock that is metamorphic. (clap, clap)

It was changed by heat and pressure

And became a different kind.

I found a rock that is metamorphic. (clap, clap)

Sing this song with children to help them become familiar with the three ways that rocks are formed. Show them an example of each rock as you sing the verses.

## Learn More About Rocks with These Books

**The Best Book of Fossils, Rocks, and Minerals**
by Chris Perrault
(Larousse Kingfisher Chambers)

**Everybody Needs a Rock**
by Byrd Baylor (Scott Foresman)

**Let's Go Rock Collecting**
by Roma Gans
(HarperCollins Juvenile Books)

**Looking at Rocks**
by Jennifer Dussling (Grosset & Dunlap)

**Rocks in His Head**
by Carol Otis Hurst (Greenwillow)

**Stone Soup**
by Ann McGovern (Scholastic)

**Sylvester and the Magic Pebble**
by William Steig (Aladdin Library)

Three Cheers for May PreK–K, SV 9825-6

# Gorgeous Geodes

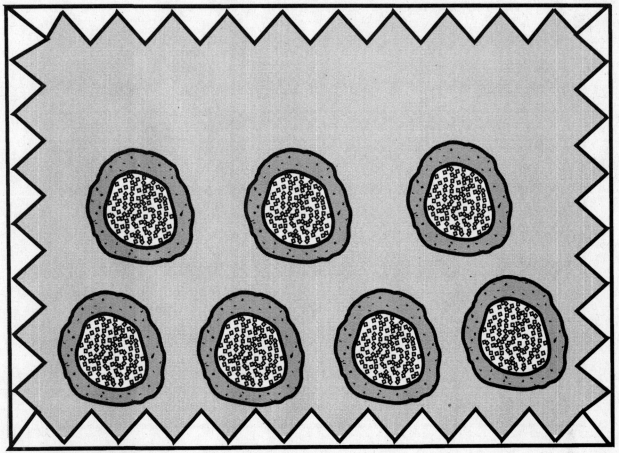

## Materials

- pattern on page 50
- craft paper
- white construction paper
- iridescent glitter
- purple, gold, silver glitter
- markers
- scissors
- glue
- a geode
- stapler

## Directions

**Teacher Preparation:** Display a geode for children to see and touch. Duplicate a copy of the geode pattern on white construction paper for each child. Mix iridescent glitter with the remaining glitter colors to give it a more sparkly effect. For information about geodes, see Teacher Information on page 41.

1. Cover the bulletin board with craft paper.

2. Cut out the geode pattern and color the outside edge with markers.

3. Cover the center of the pattern with glue and sprinkle glitter generously.

4. Arrange and staple the geodes on the board in a pleasing arrangement.

5. Add a border and caption.

Three Cheers for May PreK–K, SV 9825-6

# Rocks Are Everywhere Centers

### Art Center

**Science Standard**
Understands properties
of materials

## Rock 'n Roll

### Materials

- white construction paper
- 2 or 3 colors of tempera paint
- empty 13-ounce coffee cans with lids
- several gemstones or smooth rocks
- scissors
- 2 or 3 spoons
- 2 or 3 empty butter tubs

**Teacher Preparation:** Provide a 5" x 12" piece of construction paper for each child. Pour enough paint in each butter tub to cover the bottom. Place one or two rocks in each tub.

Have children place a piece of construction paper inside the coffee can so that it lines the inside of the can. Then have them use a spoon to thoroughly coat the rocks with paint. Scoop the rocks with the spoon and drop them in the can. Repeat with desired colors. Securely place the lid on the can. Invite children to shake the can so that the rocks "paint" the paper. Take off the lid and remove the paper. Allow the paper to dry.

### Writing Center

**Language Arts Standard**
Listens to and responds
to a variety of literature

## My Magic Pebble

### Materials

- crayons or markers
- activity master on page 54
- pencils
- *Sylvester and the Magic Pebble* by William Steig

**Teacher Preparation:** Duplicate a copy of the activity master for each child.

Read *Sylvester and the Magic Pebble* by William Steig. Discuss with children Sylvester's wish. Have them write or dictate a sentence telling what they would wish for if they had a magic pebble. Invite them to illustrate their sentence.

# Rocks Are Everywhere Centers

 ### Dramatic Play Center

**Math Standard**
Sorts or classifies by color

## Let's Be Geologists

### Materials

- sand
- sifters
- egg cartons
- plastic shovels
- straw hats, gloves
- large shallow plastic tub
- polished rocks (a few of several different colors)

**Teacher Preparation:** Fill tub half full with sand and stir in polished rocks. Make all materials available in the dramatic play center.

Lead children in a discussion about geologists, who are people that study rocks. Tell children that rocks are made up of minerals and that there are many different colors of minerals. Invite children to role-play a geologist finding rocks. Have them use shovels to fill the sifters in order to separate the rocks from the sand. Then have children sort the rocks by colors into the egg cartons.

 ### Game Center

**Math Standard**
Sequences by size

## Rock Relay

### Materials

- one plastic tub per team
- 6 different-sized rocks per team

**Teacher Preparation:** Put five rocks in each tub, leaving out one rock.

Play this sequencing game outside or in a large area of the classroom. Divide children into teams of five. Determine a starting line and a finish line for each team. Place the tub of rocks at each finish line and lay one rock near each tub. Have the first child in each line run to the tub and remove a rock. If the rock is smaller than the first rock, have the child lay it on the left side of the first rock. If it is bigger than the first rock, the child lays it to the right. Then have the child run back to the starting line. Repeat the procedure, having each child lay a rock according to its size.

**Tip:** Make sure that the sizes of the rocks in each tub are distinctly different.

# Rocks Are Everywhere Centers

### Language Center

**Language Arts Standard**
Recognizes and names uppercase and lowercase letters

## Rocks in the River

### Materials

- file folder
- one-inch-size polished rocks
- patterns on pages 51 and 52
- glue
- crayons
- scissors
- markers

**Teacher Preparation:** Duplicate a copy of each pattern. Color and cut out the left and right sides of the river. Glue them to the inside of a file folder. Write a lowercase letter on each of the rocks in the river. Write the corresponding capital letters on the polished rocks.

Have children match the capital letters to the lowercase letters.

### Math Center

**Math Standard**
Compares groups and recognizes *more than*, *less than*, and *equal to* relationships

## More or Less the Winner

### Materials

- paper cups
- plastic containers
- pattern on page 53
- 6" x 6" poster board
- pencil
- scissors
- paper clips
- 20–30 1" rocks per container
- dice
- glue
- brads

**Teacher Preparation:** Duplicate and cut out the spinner pattern. Glue it to the poster board. Use a pencil to punch a hole in the center. Insert the brad through the end of a paper clip and through the hole. Flatten the brad prongs on the back of the poster board so that the paper clip is secure but is loose enough to spin. Provide a spinner board for each partner pair.

Invite each partner to roll the die and remove that number of rocks from the container. If partners have the same number of rocks, repeat the procedure. Then have one partner spin the spinner. If the spinner points to *more than*, the partner with more rocks puts them in his or her cup. The partner with the fewer rocks returns them to the container. Continue the game until all rocks have been placed in cups. Have partners count the rocks in their cups to determine the winner.

# Rocks Are Everywhere Centers

### Science Center

**Science Standard**
Understands about scientific inquiry

## Volcano Eruption

### Materials

- measuring spoon
- 9" x 13" cake pan
- red food coloring
- 3–4 tablespoons baking soda
- dishwashing liquid
- ½ cup vinegar
- modeling clay
- measuring cup
- clean 8-ounce plastic water bottle
- water
- funnel
- newspapers

**Teacher Preparation:** Have newspapers available for cleanup.

Lead a discussion with children about volcanoes. Demonstrate this experiment to children before making it available to them at the science center. Younger children may need help with this activity.

Invite children to put the water bottle on the pan. Then have them make a volcano around the bottle with the modeling clay. Caution them not to let any of the clay get into the bottle. Have children measure the baking soda and pour it into the bottle with a funnel. Then have them measure one-half cup of water, add a few drops of dishwashing liquid, and pour both into the bottle. Ask children to measure the vinegar and mix in a few drops of red food coloring. Have them use the funnel to pour this mixture into the bottle and quickly remove the funnel. Explain that they should prepare for the eruption immediately.

### Block Center

**Math Standard**
Applies and adapts a variety of appropriate strategies to solve problems

## Rock Movers

### Materials

- toy dump truck
- generous supply of 2" to 3" rocks
- plastic tub
- large spoons

Place the rocks in a pile on the floor. Have children use the spoons to transfer the rocks from the floor to the dump truck. Invite them to drive the truck to the plastic tub and dump the rocks in the tub.

# Geode Pattern

Use with "Gorgeous Geodes" on page 45.

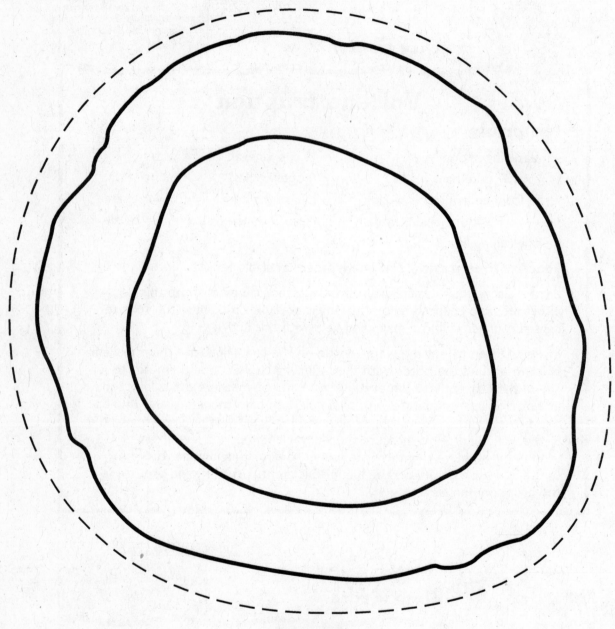

**geode**

Three Cheers for May PreK–K, SV 9825-6

# River Pattern (Left Side)

Use with "Rocks in the River" on page 48.

**left side**

Three Cheers for May PreK–K, SV 9825-6

# River Pattern (Right Side)

Use with "Rocks in the River" on page 48.

**right side**

Unit 4, Rocks Are Everywhere: Patterns
Three Cheers for May PreK–K, SV 9825-6

# Spinner Pattern

Use with "More or Less the Winner" on page 48.

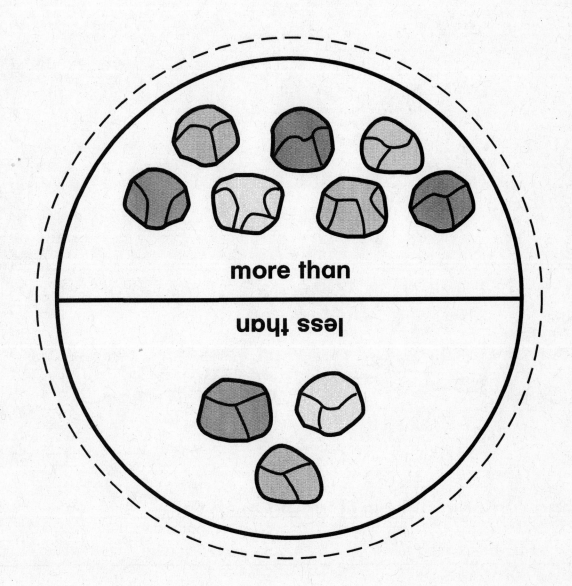

more than

less than

Three Cheers for May PreK–K, SV 9825-6

**Name** _____

# Magic Pebble Activity Master

If I had a magic pebble, I would wish for _____

_____

_____

**Directions:** Use with "My Magic Pebble" on page 46. Have children write or dictate a sentence telling what they would wish for if they had a magic pebble. Invite them to illustrate their sentence.

**54**

Unit 4, Rocks Are Everywhere: Activity Master
Three Cheers for May PreK–K, SV 9825-6

# Animal Safari

 Many animals live in the dry, tropical grasslands area known as the African savanna. It covers a large area between the tropical rain forests and the desert.

 Savannas have very warm temperatures year-round. Winter is a very long, dry season with only about 4 inches of rain. Summer is a short, wet season with up to 25 inches of rain. Between December and February there is no rain at all.

 The savanna has a large range of highly specialized plants and animals. They all depend on each other to keep environmental balance.

 Plants of the savanna have adapted so they can grow during the long periods of drought.

 The many species of plant-eating mammals coexist in one area because they have their own food preferences. Some browse or graze at different heights and at different times of the day.

 Most of the animals on the savanna have long legs or wings so that they are able to go on long migrations in search of food and water.

 Giraffes are plant eaters and spend most of their time nibbling leaves from the tops of acacia trees. They have excellent eyesight and can see long distances because of their height.

 Many of the carnivores, such as lions, do most of their hunting at night. Female lions are the hunters, but all lions rest or sleep up to 20 hours a day.

 Zebras are among the animals that graze near giraffes. The giraffes act as a warning system if danger is nearby.

 The African elephant lives in herds with only the females and their young. The herd is led by one dominant cow. Elephants have acute hearing and use their ears to fan themselves. Both males and females have tusks. The elephant's life span is about 70 years.

 Huge areas of savanna are lost to the Sahara desert every year because farmers have overgrazed their cattle and goats or farmed the land.

Three Cheers for May PreK–K, SV 9825-6

# Animal Finger Puppets

## Materials

- patterns on page 64
- scissors
- tape
- crayons

## Directions

**Teacher Preparation:** Duplicate a copy of the finger puppets for each child. Lead a discussion with children about animals that they might see while on a safari.

1. Color the animals and cut out the finger puppets.

2. Tape the tabs together and wear.

# Safari Binoculars

## Materials

- a pair of binoculars
- construction paper
- scissors
- markers
- glue
- yarn
- hole punch
- empty bathroom tissue tubes (2 per child)
- stapler

## Directions

**Teacher Preparation:** Staple the two tubes together. Cut construction paper to fit around the tubes. Lead a discussion with children about how binoculars make objects look closer and clearer. Invite children to look through a pair of binoculars.

1. Use markers to decorate the construction paper. Glue the paper around the tubes.

2. Punch a hole on each side of one end of the tubes. Attach yarn to the two holes.

3. Wear around your neck. Look through your binoculars!

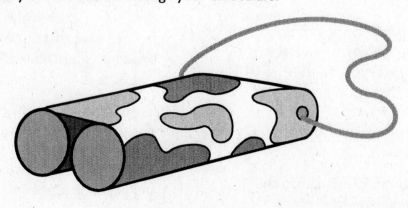

Three Cheers for May PreK–K, SV 9825-6

# Zebra Cakes

## You will need

- rice cakes
- cream cheese
- raisins
- paper plates
- plastic knives

## Directions

1. Use a plastic knife to cover the top of the rice cake with cream cheese.

2. Place raisins across the cream cheese so that they look like zebra stripes.

3. Eat and enjoy!

Three Cheers for May PreK–K, SV 9825-6

# ♫ Goin' on a Safari

(Tune: "Here We Go 'Round the Mulberry Bush")

Here we go on a safari, a safari, a safari.

Here we go on a safari,

What animals will we see?

There goes a lion, a lion, a lion.

There goes a lion.

Listen to him roar.

(roar)

There goes a giraffe, a giraffe, a giraffe.

There goes a giraffe.

See him stand so tall.

(stretch)

There goes a zebra, a zebra, a zebra.

There goes a zebra.

Count his many stripes.

(count to 10)

There goes an elephant, an elephant, an elephant.

There goes an elephant.

See him raise his trunk.

(clasp hands together and raise above head)

## Go on a Safari with These Stories

**African Animals**
by Caroline Arnold (William Morrow)

**African Animals ABC: An Alphabet Safari**
by Sarah L. Schuette (Pebble Books)

**Here Is the African Savanna**
by Madeline Dunphy (Hyperion Press)

**The Elephant's Child**
by Rudyard Kipling (Voyager Books)

**We All Went on a Safari: A Counting Journey Through Tanzania**
by Laurie Krebs (Barefoot Books)

**The Whole Night Through: A Lullaby**
by David Frampton (HarperCollins)

**Zella, Zack, and Zodiac**
by Bill Peet (Houghton Mifflin Co.)

# Zany Zebras

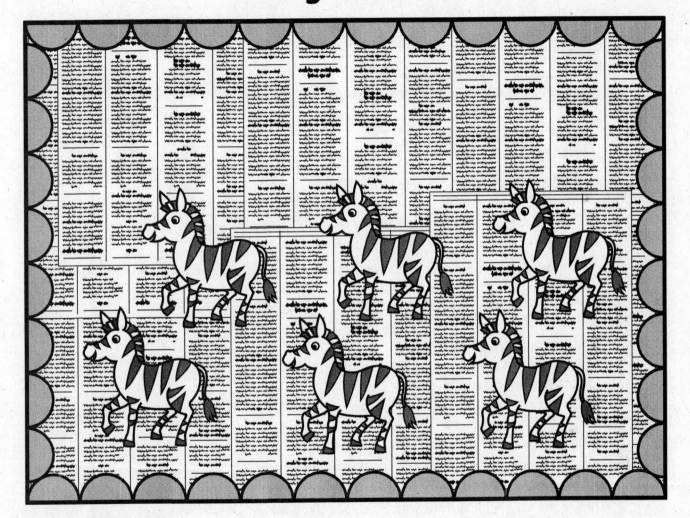

## Materials

- pattern on page 65
- newspapers
- white construction paper
- black tempera paint
- small paintbrushes
- wiggly eyes
- scissors
- stapler
- glue

## Directions

**Teacher Preparation:** Duplicate the zebra pattern on white construction paper. Provide a copy for each child. Cover the bulletin board with the classified sections of the newspaper that have no photos. Discuss with children how camouflage provides protection for animals.

1. Cut out and paint black stripes on the zebra.

2. Glue on a wiggly eye.

3. Arrange and staple the zebras in a pleasing arrangement on the bulletin board.

4. Add a festive border and the caption.

Three Cheers for May PreK–K, SV 9825-6

# Animal Safari Centers

### Art Center

**Science Standards**
Understands properties
of materials

## Lion Mask

### Materials

- elastic cord
- watercolor paints
- 9-inch paper plates
- patterns on page 66
- paintbrushes
- pony beads
- hole punch
- brown construction paper
- glue
- stapler
- scissors

**Teacher Preparation:** Cut out the patterns to use as templates. Trace the mask template on a paper plate. Cut out the mask and the eye holes. Provide a paper plate mask and an ear template for each child. Cut 10" strips of elastic cord and provide one for each child.

1. Paint the mask yellow.
2. Trace the ear template on brown construction paper and cut out two ears. Staple the ears to the mask.
3. Cut several 1" x 3" strips of brown paper. Glue them around the edge of the mask for the lion's mane.
4. Punch a hole on each side of the mask.
5. Thread each end of the elastic cord through a punched hole in the mask and through one bead. Tie a knot to secure.

Paint the tip of child's nose with black paint and add black whiskers.

### Block Center

**Language Arts Standard**
Writes labels and captions

## Name the Animals

### Materials

- markers
- index cards
- blocks
- plastic African animals

Have children sort the animals. Then invite them to build pens for the animals. Challenge them to make a sign that names each animal.

# Animal Safari Centers

 **Dramatic Play Center**

**Language Arts Standard**
Writes words that move left to right

## Go on a Safari

### Materials

- masking tape
- tempera paints
- large appliance box
- binoculars (made in "Safari Binoculars" on page 56)
- toy cameras
- box cutter
- paintbrush
- pencils
- clipboard
- straw hats
- paper

**Teacher Preparation:** Lay the box on its side and tape the ends shut. Cut out a section on top that is large enough to place one or two chairs inside the box. Then cut a door on each side. Paint the box to look like a safari vehicle.

Invite children to sit in the "vehicle" and role-play looking for animals. Have them use the binoculars and the cameras. Encourage them to make a list of the animals that they see.

 **Language Center**

**Language Arts Standard**
Knows the sounds of the letters of the alphabet

## Name the Sound

### Materials

- file folder
- black marker
- cards on page 67
- crayons
- scissors
- white construction paper

**Teacher Preparation:** Duplicate on construction paper, color, and cut apart the cards. Write the first letter of the name of each animal on the inside of the file folder. Space the letters evenly and draw grass and trees around them. You may wish to cut off the names from the cards before placing the cards in the center.

Have children place the animal card on the letter that makes the beginning sound of the animal's name.

# Animal Safari Centers

### Math Center

**Math Standard**
Associates numerals up to 10 with sets of objects

## How Many?

### Materials

- pencils
- crayons
- activity master on page 68

**Teacher Preparation:** Duplicate a copy of the activity master for each child.

Have children count the animals in each box and circle the correct number. Encourage children to color the animals.

### Puzzle Center

**Math Standard**
Matches objects to outlines of shapes

## Safari Puzzle

### Materials

- pattern on page 69
- white construction paper
- crayons
- scissors

**Teacher Preparation:** Duplicate the animal picture on construction paper. Color and cut the picture into five or six puzzle pieces.

Have children put the puzzle together.

# Animal Safari Centers

 **Sensory Center**

**Science Standard**
Understands characteristics
of organisms

## Camouflaged Animals

### Materials

- rice
- large plastic tub
- small plastic animals such as lions, giraffes, zebras, hippopotamuses, leopards, and elephants

**Teacher Preparation:** Place the animals on the bottom of the sensory tub. Fill the tub with rice.

Invite children to find the animals. Challenge them to identify the animals and name them by touch before pulling them out of the tub.

 **Writing Center**

**Language Arts Standard**
Makes illustrations to match
sentences

## My Favorite Animal

### Materials

- pencils
- crayons
- activity master on page 70

**Teacher Preparation:** Duplicate a copy of the activity master for each child.

Lead a discussion with children about the animals that they might see while on a safari. Invite them to draw a picture of their favorite safari animal. Then have children write or dictate an answer to complete the sentence.

Three Cheers for May PreK–K, SV 9825-6

# Puppet Patterns

Use with "Animal Finger Puppets" on page 56.

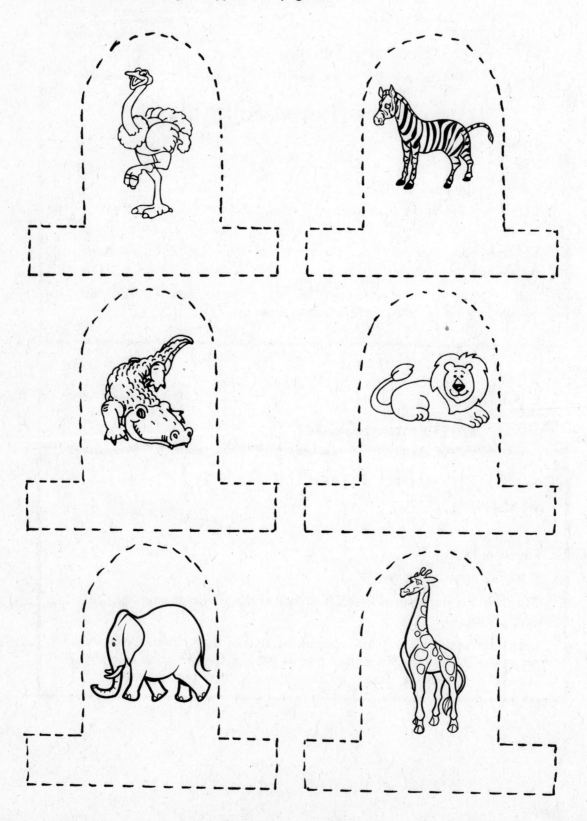

Unit 5, Animal Safari: Patterns
Three Cheers for May PreK–K, SV 9825-6

# Zebra Pattern

Use with "Zany Zebras" on page 59.

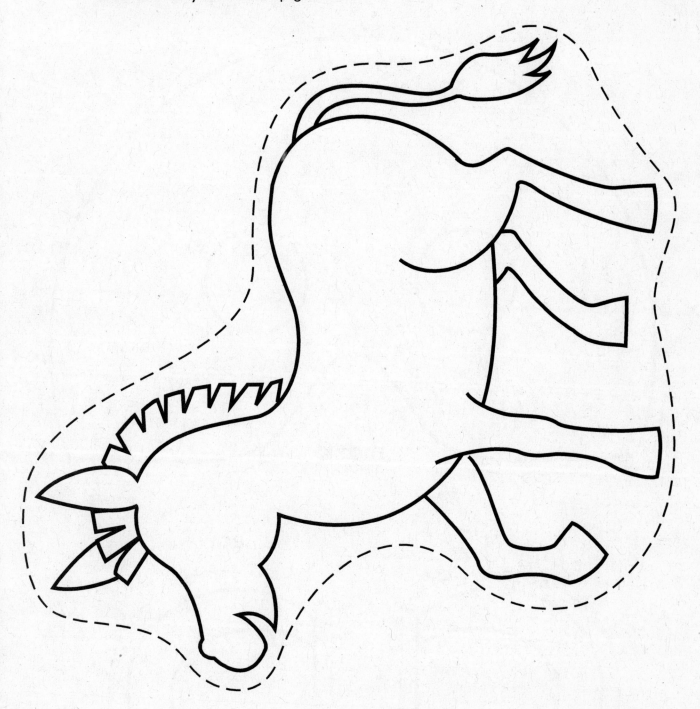

Three Cheers for May PreK–K, SV 9825-6

# Mask and Ears Patterns

Use with "Lion Mask" on page 60.

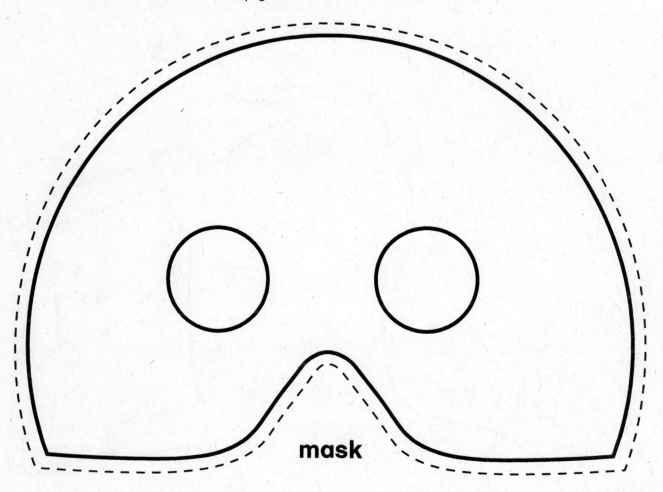

mask

ear           ear

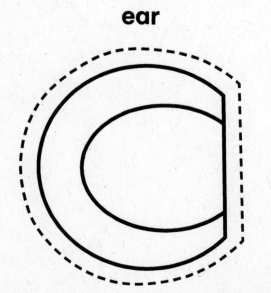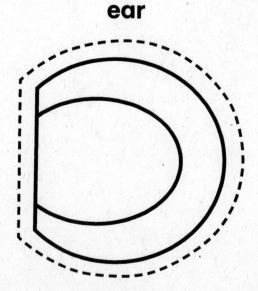

Unit 5, Animal Safari: Patterns

Three Cheers for May PreK–K, SV 9825-6

# Animal Cards

Use with "Name the Sound" on page 61.

lion

elephant

hippopotamus

gorilla

zebra

crocodile

ostrich

flamingo

Unit 5, Animal Safari: Cards
Three Cheers for May PreK–K, SV 9825-6

# Name _____

# Counting

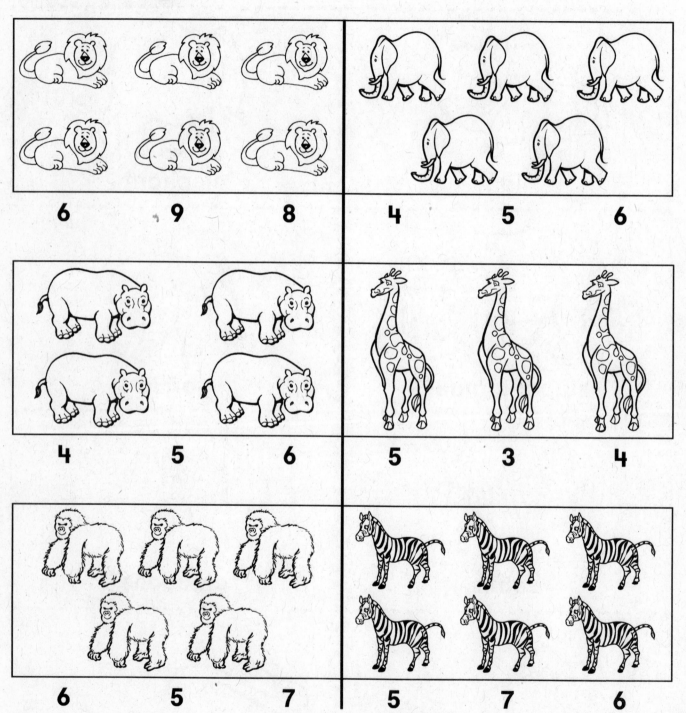

| | | |
|---|---|---|
| 6   9   8 | 4   5   6 |
| 4   5   6 | 5   3   4 |
| 6   5   7 | 5   7   6 |

**Directions:** Use with "How Many?" on page 62. Have children count the animals in each box and circle the correct number. Encourage children to color the animals.

**Unit 5, Animal Safari: Activity Master**
Three Cheers for May PreK–K, SV 9825-6

# Puzzle Pattern

Use with "Safari Puzzle" on page 62.

Unit 5, Animal Safari: Patterns
Three Cheers for May PreK–K, SV 9825-6

**Name** _____

# Favorite Animal

My favorite animal is

_____

_____

because _____

_____

**Directions:** Use with "My Favorite Animal" on page 63. Invite children to draw a picture of their favorite safari animal. Then have children write or dictate an answer to complete the sentence.

Unit 5, Animal Safari: Activity Master
Three Cheers for May PreK–K, SV 9825-6

# Celebrate with Mexico

 Mexico is the country directly south of the United States. Mexico borders California, New Mexico, Arizona, and Texas.

 The dominant language in Mexico is Spanish.

 The flag of Mexico is divided into three vertical sections. The first section is green, which symbolizes hope. The middle section is white, which symbolizes purity. The third section is red, which symbolizes the blood shed during the fight for independence.

 In the center of the Mexican flag and on the coat of arms of Mexico is an eagle on a cactus.

 The family is the first priority for people of Mexico. Children are celebrated and sheltered by their families.

 Mexican cuisine often revolves around three main food items, which are tortillas, fried beans, and chili peppers.

 Mariachi music is one of the most well-known styles of music in Mexico. A complete mariachi band consists of violins, trumpets, and guitars. This type of music is played for many types of celebrations.

 The people of Mexico acknowledge important historical or religious dates with celebrations or fiestas. Many Hispanic Americans also observe major Mexican holidays.

 Cinco de Mayo is a regional holiday that commemorates Mexico's victory over an invading French army on May 5, 1862.

 A favorite activity for children at fiestas or celebrations is the breaking of a piñata. The piñata is a brightly decorated paper or clay container filled with candy and toys. It is hung from the ceiling or a tree. Children are blindfolded and attempt to break the piñata with a stick in order to retrieve the treats.

**71**

Unit 6, Celebrate with Mexico: Teacher Information
Three Cheers for May PreK–K, SV 9825-6

# A Personal Piñata

## Materials

- lunch sacks
- brightly colored tissue paper
- wrapped candy and stickers
- newspaper
- scissors
- glue
- stapler
- yarn
- hole punch

## Directions

**Teacher Preparation:** Cut tissue paper into 2" x 5" strips. Stuff sacks with newspaper so that the sacks will stand upright while the children cover them with tissue paper. Have children practice using scissors to fringe paper strips. Provide a paper sack for each child.

1. Fringe tissue paper strips with scissors.

2. Begin at the bottom of the sack and use glue to cover one side with fringed strips. Overlap the strips so that the sack is completely covered.

3. Repeat the procedure on the opposite side of the sack.

4. Remove the newspaper from the sack and fill with desired treats.

5. Fold over top of sack twice and staple.

6. Punch two holes on the folded section. Loop yarn through the holes and tie ends together.

7. Hang piñatas from ceiling, if desired.

---

# A Pretty Poncho

## Materials

- white craft paper
- black permanent marker
- scissors
- paintbrushes
- tempera paints (bright colors)

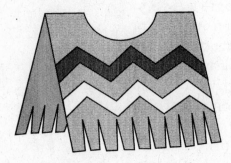

## Directions

**Teacher Preparation:** Cut a 16" x 36" piece of white craft paper for each child and fold each piece in half. Cut a hole for child's head on the fold. For younger children, draw lines, such as zigzags, across both sides of the paper to use as guidelines for painting.

1. Use scissors to fringe the top and bottom ends of the paper.

2. Lay the paper flat and paint bright stripes on the front and back sides.

3. Allow paint to dry. Wear poncho to role-play in dramatic play center on page 76.

Three Cheers for May PreK–K, SV 9825-6

# Buenos Burritos

## You will need

- flour tortillas (one per child)
- can of refried beans
- shredded cheese
- picante sauce or salsa
- can opener
- paper plates
- toothpicks
- plastic spoons, knives
- microwave oven

## Directions

**Teacher Preparation:** Prepare ingredients for serving.

1. Spread refried beans in the center of the tortilla.
2. Add cheese and sauce.
3. Wrap tortilla around ingredients and secure with a toothpick.
4. Warm for 10–15 seconds in the microwave.

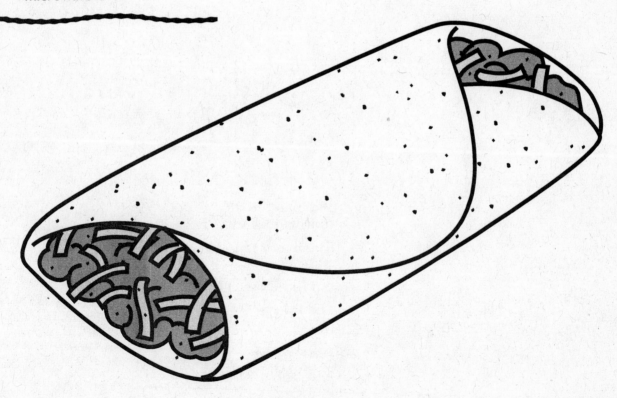

Three Cheers for May PreK–K, SV 9825-6

# ♫ Ten Friends

(Tune: "Ten Little Indians")

Uno, dos, tres amigos.

Cuatro, cinco, seis amigos.

Siete, ocho, nueve amigos.

Diez amigos.

## Celebrate Mexico with These Books

**Borreguita and the Coyote**
by Verna Aardema
(Random House Children's Books)

**Cinco de Mayo**
by Janet Riehecky (Children's Press)

**Cinco de Mayo (Rookie Read-About Holidays)**
by Mary Dodson Wade (Children's Press)

**The Piñata Maker**
by George Ancona (Harcourt Children's Books)

**Postcards from Mexico**
by Helen Arnold (Zoe Books)

**Saturday Market**
by Patricia Grossman (HarperCollins)

**The Tortilla Factory**
by Gary Paulsen (Voyager Books)

# Mexican Bark Paintings

## Materials

- blue craft paper
- brown grocery bags
- black permanent marker
- oil pastels or colored chalk
- bark painting examples
- stapler

## Directions

**Teacher Preparation:** Cover the bulletin board with craft paper. Tear flat sides off of grocery bag. One bag will yield two flat sections.

Lead a discussion with children about people in Mexico who paint pictures on thin pieces of bark. Point out that they often draw things that are seen in nature. Display examples of bark paintings.

1. Draw a simple picture on a torn section of the grocery bag with black permanent marker. Include a decorative border. Younger children may need help with the drawings.

2. Crumple the paper into a ball to give it a bark-like texture.

3. Smooth out and lay the paper flat on the table.

4. Color each part of the drawing with bright colored chalk or oil pastels. Use a variety of colors.

Arrange and staple "bark" drawings in a pleasing arrangement on the bulletin board. Add a festive border and the caption.

Three Cheers for May PreK–K, SV 9825-6

# Celebrate with Mexico Centers

### Art Center

**Social Studies Standard**
Identifies customs and traditions

## Flag of Mexico

### Materials

- markers
- pattern on page 80
- picture of the flag of Mexico
- red and green tissue paper squares
- glue
- globe
- scissors

**Teacher Preparation:** Duplicate a copy of the flag for each child.

Have children locate Mexico on the globe. Discuss with them the colors and symbols on the Mexican flag. Invite children to cover the two sections of the flag with red and green tissue paper. Then have them color the symbols.

### Dramatic Play Center

**Social Studies Standard**
Identifies customs associated with holidays

## Cinco de Mayo Celebration

### Materials

- colorful skirts, serapes, and vests
- tissue paper flowers with hair clips
- ponchos (made in "A Pretty Poncho" on page 72)
- sombreros
- toy guitar, maracas
- lively Mexican music

**Teacher Preparation:** Lead a discussion with children about how people celebrate Cinco de Mayo. See Teacher Information on page 71. Invite children to role-play a Cinco de Mayo celebration. Encourage them to play the instruments and dance to the music.

# Celebrate with Mexico Centers

### Game Center

**Social Studies Standard**
Follows rules such as taking turns

## Circle Countdown

### Materials

• none

Have children practice counting to ten in Spanish. Then have them stand in a circle with the teacher in the middle. Invite one child to pick a number as the featured number. For example, number five (cinco) is the featured number picked. Beginning with the child who picked the number, have children count to five (or the featured number) in Spanish with the teacher pointing to the next child in the circle for each number. Have each fifth child sit down. Continue until one child is left standing.

### Language Center

**Language Arts Standard**
Counts the number of syllables in a word

## How Many Claps?

### Materials

• pencils
• crayons
• activity master on page 81

**Teacher Preparation:** Duplicate a copy of the activity master for each child.

Have children practice naming the items on the activity master using the Spanish words. In the center, have them say each word and clap for each syllable. For example, a-(clap) mi-(clap) gos- (clap) has three claps for three syllables. Invite children to write the number of claps in each word and color the pictures.

# Celebrate with Mexico Centers

## Math Center

**Math Standard**
Reads numbers to 10

## Colorful Piñata

### Materials

- crayons
- activity master on page 82

**Teacher Preparation:** Provide a copy of the activity master for each child. Prepare a chart that shows which color to use for each number: 1 = blue, 2 = green, 3 = yellow, 4 = red, 5 = orange, and 6 = black. Display the chart in the math center.

Have children color the piñata using the color code.

## Music Center

**Social Studies Standard**
Identifies customs associated with holidays

## Musical Maracas

### Materials

- dry beans
- patterns on page 83
- empty pint-sized milk cartons
- glue
- stapler
- craft sticks
- lively Mexican music
- crayons
- scissors

**Teacher Preparation:** Duplicate a copy of the patterns for each child. Thoroughly rinse the milk cartons and allow to dry.

Invite the children to color the pictures. Then have them cut out the four boxes and glue them upside down on the sides of the milk carton. Have children place a small handful of beans inside the carton, add a craft stick to the opening, and staple closed. Play lively Mexican music and have children shake the maracas to the beat.

# Celebrate with Mexico Centers

### Sensory Center

**Social Studies Standard**
Identifies customs and traditions

## Play Dough Tortillas

### Materials

- white play dough
- plastic place mats
- *The Tortilla Factory* by Gary Paulsen
- rolling pins
- tortilla press

Read *The Tortilla Factory* by Gary Paulsen. Invite children to roll the play dough into a ball. Then have them place it on the tortilla press and flatten the ball to make a tortilla. The play dough can be flattened with a rolling pin if a press is not available.

### Writing Center

**Language Arts Standard**
Writes words that move left to right

## *Amigos* Means Friends

### Materials

- pencils
- crayons
- activity master on page 84

**Teacher Preparation:** Duplicate a copy of the activity master for each child.

Introduce children to the Spanish words *mis amigos*. Tell them that the words mean *my friends*. Place a chart in the center with the names of the children who are in your classroom.

Have children write the names of five of their friends from the classroom.

# Flag Pattern

Use with "Flag of Mexico" on page 76.

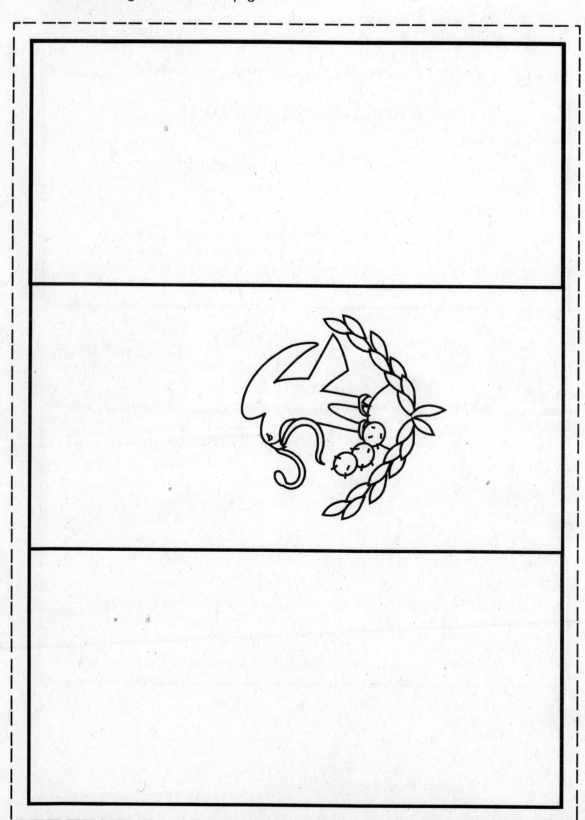

Three Cheers for May PreK–K, SV 9825-6

**Name** _____

# Syllables

sombrero

_____
- - - - - - - - - - - - -
_____

piñata

_____
- - - - - - - - - - - - -
_____

maracas

_____
- - - - - - - - - - - - -
_____

amigos

_____
- - - - - - - - - - - - -
_____

**Directions:** Use with "How Many Claps?" on page 77. Have children practice naming the items using the Spanish words. Invite children to write the number of claps in each word and color the pictures.

Unit 6, Celebrate with Mexico: Activity Master
Three Cheers for May PreK–K, SV 9825-6

**Name** _____

# Piñata

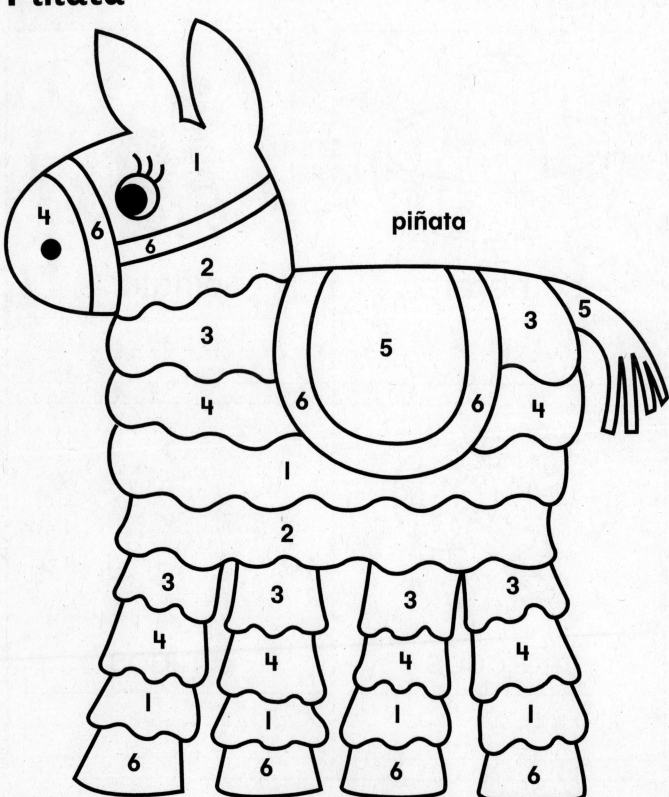

piñata

**Directions:** Use with "Colorful Piñata" on page 78. Have children color the piñata using the color code.

Unit 6, Celebrate with Mexico: Activity Master
Three Cheers for May PreK–K, SV 9825-6

# Maraca Patterns

Use with "Musical Maracas" on page 78.

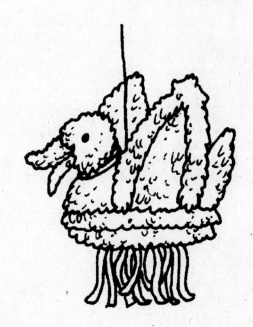

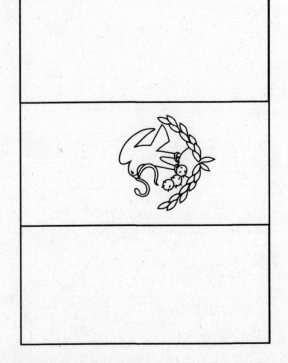

Unit 6, Celebrate with Mexico: Patterns
Three Cheers for May PreK–K, SV 9825-6

**Name** _____

# Friends

## Mis amigos

_____

1. _____

2. _____

3. _____

4. _____

5. _____

**Directions:** Use with "*Amigos* Means Friends" on page 79. Have children write the names of five of their friends from the classroom.

Three Cheers for May PreK–K, SV 9825-6

# A Look at Eve Bunting

 Eve Bunting was born on December 19, 1928, in Magnera, Ireland.

 She grew up in an environment filled with tales of ghosts and fairies and of old Irish heroes.

 In 1958, at the age of thirty, Eve Bunting moved to California with her husband and three children.

 Several years later she enrolled in a community college creative writing course.

 Her first book was published in 1972. *The Two Giants* was a retelling of a folktale that she knew from her childhood.

 Since that first book, Eve Bunting has written more than one hundred others. Her books are written for audiences of all ages, ranging from preschool to young adults.

 One of her greatest joys is writing picture books that tell stories of happiness or sorrow with just a few simple words.

 She often writes picture books that make children question why things happen. Many of her books address difficult issues, including racial prejudice, death, war, and troubled families.

 She also writes books that are pure fun, such as *Sunflower House, Happy Birthday, Dear Duck,* and *Scary, Scary Halloween.*

 Eve Bunting has received many awards and honors, including the Golden Kite Award from the Society of Children's Book Writers in 1976 for *One More Flight.*

**Unit 7, Author Study: Teacher Information**
Three Cheers for May PreK–K, SV 9825-6

# Literature Selection: *The Mother's Day Mice* by Eve Bunting

In honor of Mother's Day read *The Mother's Day Mice*. Have children think of something special that they can do for someone they love on Mother's Day that does not cost money. Invite them to make a special card or a corsage using the directions below.

## Tissue Paper Corsage

### Materials

- pattern on page 89
- white poster board
- pin backings
- 2" squares of brightly colored tissue paper
- 1" yellow pom-poms
- hot glue gun
- glue
- scissors
- pencils

### Directions

**Teacher Preparation:** Trace the pattern on the white poster board and cut it out. Provide one for each child. Glue a pin backing on each flower. Provide a generous supply of tissue paper squares.

Have children glue the yellow pom-pom in the center of the flower. Then have them wrap one tissue paper square on the eraser end of a pencil and apply a small dot of glue to the center of the square. Use the pencil to press the tissue square onto the flower shape. Repeat the procedure until the flower is completely covered with tissue paper squares.

## Mother's Day Card

### Materials

- pattern on page 90
- activity master on page 91
- scissors
- glue
- crayons
- 9" x 12" construction paper (spring colors)

### Directions

**Teacher Preparation:** Duplicate a copy of the pattern and the activity master for each child.

Have children decorate the pattern on page 90 and cut it out. Then have them fold a piece of construction paper in half and glue the picture on the front to make a Mother's Day card. Invite them to dictate or write responses to complete the sentences on the activity master on page 91. Have children cut out and glue the responses to the inside of the card.

# Books by Eve Bunting

- *A Day's Work* (Houghton Mifflin Company)

- *Butterfly House* (Scholastic)

- *Dandelions* (Voyager Books)

- *Flower Garden* (Voyager Books)

- *Going Home* (HarperTrophy)

- *Happy Birthday, Dear Duck* (Clarion Books)

- *I Love You, Too!* (Cartwheel Books)

- *The Mother's Day Mice* (Clarion Books)

- *Night Tree* (Voyager Books)

- *St. Patrick's Day in the Morning* (Clarion Books)

- *Scary, Scary Halloween* (Clarion Books)

- *Someday a Tree* (Clarion Books)

- *Sunflower House* (Voyager Books)

- *The Valentine Bears* (Clarion Books)

- *The Wednesday Surprise* (Scott Foresman)

Unit 7, Author Study: Book List
Three Cheers for May PreK–K, SV 9825-6

# Bookmark Patterns

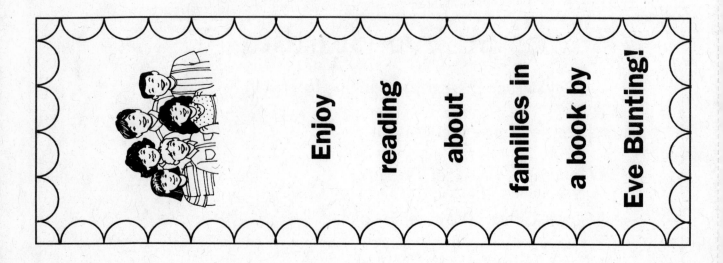

Enjoy reading about families in a book by Eve Bunting!

Celebrate Mother's Day with a book by Eve Bunting!

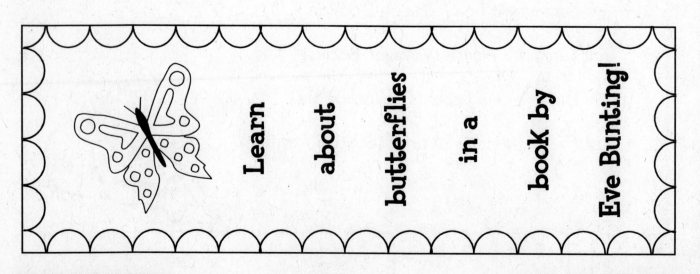

Learn about butterflies in a book by Eve Bunting!

Unit 7, Author Study: Patterns
Three Cheers for May PreK–K, SV 9825-6

# Corsage Pattern

Use with "Tissue Paper Corsage" on page 86.

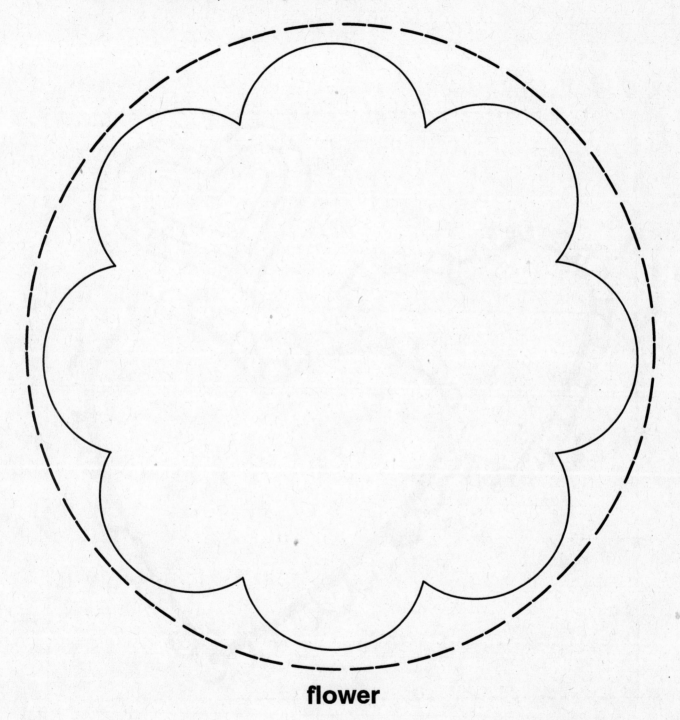

**flower**

**89**

Unit 7, Author Study: Pattern
Three Cheers for May PreK–K, SV 9825-6

# Card Pattern

Use with "Mother's Day Card" on page 86.

Three Cheers for May PreK–K, SV 9825-6

**Name** _____

# My Special Person

My special person's name is _____.

Her favorite color is _____.

She likes to wear _____.

She likes to go _____.

I like it when she _____.

I would like to buy her _____.

Love,

_____

**Directions:** Use with "Mother's Day Card" on page 86. Invite children to dictate or write responses to complete the sentences. Have children cut out and glue the responses on the inside of the card on page 90.

Three Cheers for May PreK–K, SV 9825-6

# Center Icons Patterns

**Art Center**

**Block Center**

**Dramatic Play Center**

**Game Center**

# Center Icons Patterns

**Language Center**

**Math Center**

**Music Center**

**Puzzle Center**

**Center Icons Patterns**
Three Cheers for May PreK–K, SV 9825-6

# Center Icons Patterns

**Reading Center**

**Science Center**

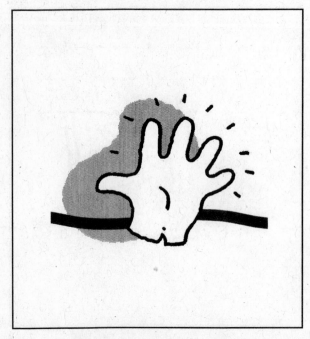

**Sensory Center**

**Writing Center**

Three Cheers for May PreK–K, SV 9825-6

# Student Awards

It's time to blast off!

_____

- - - - - - - - - - - - - -

_____

**Child's name**

### did a great job in

_____

- - - - - - - - - - - - - -

_____ .

**Teacher's signature**        **Date**

_____

- - - - - - - - - - - - - -

_____

**Child's name**

### Congratulations,

### You are the May
### Student of the Month for

_____

- - - - - - - - - - - - - -

_____ .

**Teacher's signature**        **Date**

**Student Awards Patterns**
Three Cheers for May PreK–K, SV 9825-6

# Student Award

## The jungle is swinging over

_____

- - - - - - - - - - - - - - - - - - 's

**Child's name**

## good behavior.

_____
**Teacher's signature**

_____
**Date**

# Calendar Day Pattern

**Suggested Uses**

- Reproduce one card for each day of the month. Write a numeral on each card and place it on your class calendar. Use cards to mark special days.
- Reproduce to make cards to use in word ladders or word walls.
- Reproduce to make cards and write a letter on each card. Children use the cards to form words.
- Reproduce to make cards to create matching or concentration games for students to use in activity centers. Choose from the following possible matching skills or create your own:
  — uppercase and lowercase letters
  — pictures of objects whose names rhyme, have the same beginning or ending sounds, contain short or long vowels
  — pictures of adult animals and baby animals
  — numerals and pictures of objects
  — number words and numerals
  — colors and shapes
  — high-frequency sight words

Three Cheers for May PreK–K, SV 9825-6